Boychik Poems

poems by

Barry Vitcov

Finishing Line Press
Georgetown, Kentucky

Boychik Poems

Dedicated to my grandparents,
David and Frances Blechman
&
Sam and Libby Vitcov,
for all their food and stories,
which continue to nourish my imagination.

ACKNOWLEDGMENTS

"Time Passes" in *The Drabble*
"Orange Groves in Israel" in *Ink Pantry*
 "A Redheaded Girl" and "Jewball" in *The Jefferson Journal*

Publisher: Leah Huete de Maines
Editor: Christen Kincaid
Cover Art: Barry Vitcov
Author Photo: William E. Saltzstein
Cover Design: Elizabeth Maines McCleavy

Order online: www.finishinglinepress.com
also available on amazon.com

Author inquiries and mail orders:
Finishing Line Press
PO Box 1626
Georgetown, Kentucky 40324
USA

Contents

Words should be weighed, not counted.
Yiddish Proverb

My Song

my song

is a breath
in millennia

inhaled
and
exhaled

Love Does Not Choose

Who said we were a people chosen
and then left us not feeling chosen?

Like when we stood along the baseline
hoping we were not the last chosen,

or the time we anxiously waited
for the notice that we were chosen

by a college to which we applied
disappointed we were not chosen.

Emotions run high when decisions
depend on whether we are chosen.

Those were simple lessons preparing
us for a life of the unchosen,

when love came along out of nowhere
we believed a time to be chosen

and all the Fates seemed to be aligned.
It takes more than love to be chosen.

Orange Groves in Israel

Orange groves in Israel...
my grandparents donated trees
for every special occasion,
circumcisions, birthdays, anniversaries,
bar mitzvahs,
when Kennedy became president,
the moon landing

You'll visit one day
say shalom to your forest of fruit

And they bought Israeli bonds
at the Bank of America on Irving St.
whenever they could accumulate
25 or 50 dollars

Redeem them for college
no car, nothing frivolous

Citrus and scholarship
recipe for a meaningful life
Jews have a long tradition
with fruit and words
and long arguments over
their meaning and importance

When my Aunt Sylvia
left one shul to join another
because one excluded and not the other
it might be said it was over oranges
a symbol of a more inclusive community
where segments make a whole
where the sweetness of humanity
is ascribed in its words

Chanukah Memories

We were chasing holidays like rainbows,
clues beneath colorful wrapping papers,
satin ribbons pulled as excitement grows
with scents of indescribable vapors:
those memories of Bubbe's chicken soup,
kasha varnishkes and slow cooked brisket,
honey cake and latkes that do not droop.
Playing games without being complicit
with first cousins teamed against my sisters.
The dreidel spinning for raisins and nuts,
winning the pot with laughter and whispers.
Adults admonish, "Do not utter putz."
This time is not captured when others sing
these are a few of my favorite things.

My Bar Mitzvah After Party

My father, grandfather and great grandfather
in their finest dark suits and serious faces
taking turns chanting their aliyoth
while all I want is survival
and approbation.

When it's done, the Torah
paraded, kissed, placed back in the ark
beneath an eternal flame,
the whole mishpachah
returns to our home
where mother, grandmother, great grandmother
have laid the table with meats and sweets.

Before eating, shot glasses are filled,
a toast made to my becoming a man
while I collect envelopes filled with gelt
and receive hugs from bosomy, perfumed aunts
that go on a little too long,
handshakes and mazel tov from uncles
who smile with secrets I'll never know.

My family celebrates with stories, advice,
off-color humor, reminders of antisemitism,
the purchase of Israeli bonds and trees,
and the mandate of education regardless of motivation.
Nothing is more important than whispered admonition.

The party goes on with too much wine and whiskey
for one uncle who's removed to the back patio
by his brothers and hosed down to soaked sobriety.
The most lasting memory for a newly-minted man
is a drenched drunk uncle at the after-party.

From the Point of View of a Jew
Who Embraces a Poodle Puppy

Crescent moon hangs silent
            in a warm night sky
while my poodle puppy
            hops like a hora
with joy and investigation
            of a smaller, more intimate universe
her music unlike the moon's
            more animated, less introspective

I remember bubbe lighting the shabbat candelabra
            flickering before the sweet scent of challah
her reminder to gather with kindness
            Zaide chants Baruch atah Adonai Eloheinu
today I dip my finger into sweet wine
            offering a taste to the puppy
we wait for roasted chicken and brisket
            hungry for ancient memories

Some taught, some experienced
            accumulated wisdom, myths and truths
sorting becomes labored with age
            my poodle's reality a scent,
a taste, a snuggle, a chew
            basic necessities and realities
from the point of view of a Jew
            who embraces a poodle puppy

Danced Like a Greek

Mother was a terrible cook.
Every dinner was an exercise
in where-can-I-hide-the-mushy-peas,
boiled gray without any nutritional value
like wads of indigestible cardboard.
She danced in an unkempt kitchen
saluting her surroundings
like a Greek goddess fallen from an urn,
her stage a frying pan without purpose.
She wasn't a dreamer or a pragmatist,
life in purgatory between bliss and utility.
She was simply distracted by children
and a violent husband who wasn't physical
but the emotional threat was always present.
And so she danced with jars of joy
with the pretense of meals
left to our imagination.

Grandpa's Sandwiches

He taught me about sandwiches
fundamental lessons
kosher salami and Swiss
not very kosher
and always on rye bread
with a good spicy mustard
although French's is always okay
crisp dill pickle on the meat side
not the cheese
only the meat

Boychik
there's a right way
and a wrong way
always keep that in mind

Now onion sandwiches are much simpler
thinly sliced white onion
between two slices of white bread
no condiments necessary
although butter can be used
(It's something the French like.)
use the kind of bread
you can ball up
and chew on like sugary dessert

Boychik
the onions will put
hair on your chest
you won't regret it
until you turn gray

Now let's talk about sardines
only the ones packed in olive oil
add them to an onion sandwich
forget the idea of butter
sardines, onions, white bread
one of the great joys in life

Boychik
I'll have a Falstaff
Birerly's orange for you
there's a right way
and a wrong way
always keep that in mind

Bubbe

Bubbe ain't what you think
Two hundred round bosomy pounds
cheap seltzer-spritzed wine at hand
Whole chickens with feet attached
Rinsed carrots, celery, pealed chunks of onion,
bay leaves, garlic
Always simmering on the O'Keefe and Merritt
Nu boychik?
Blue eyes glimmering with laughter
Numbers tattooed on her forearm
A hungry life no more
Not much Bubbe

New Year's at Grandma's

The New Year passed without any drama,
no fireworks, family quarrels, no booze,
unless you count the demise of grandma
when we were all taking a post-meal snooze.

She didn't die or anything like that,
although in retrospect it might have been
a better fate than the one she begat,
a former life of sordid, lustful sin.

Grandchildren, looking where they should not look,
were nosing in nana's dresser drawers
when they discovered an ancient scrapbook
with pictures best left behind closed doors.

Ensuing questions are not always best
if memories are meant to be at rest.

The Waiting Room

what do we notice
when entering an
empty waiting room
empty chairs lined in a
straight-backed void
the faces of hope or despair
having already left
with diagnoses and prescriptions

entering hand-in-hand
both of us nervous
about to lay a future
on an examination table
never warm enough

remembering when parents
informed us of their end of days
with the solemnity of age
and the humor of their years

the chairs seem emptier
if emptiness could be less
when entering an
empty waiting room

A Redheaded Girl

born at a time to wonder
about the numbers on her arm
too young to ask about memories
when we played on the steps
of my great-grandfather's apartment house

your redheaded joy never
hinting at the brutality you survived
you survived for all of us
to carry a historical burden
not understood as a child

felt deeply as an adult
responsible to know and share
over and over and over
inward and outward sensibilities

because freckled girls
and curly-haired boys
may never laugh together again
but need to make sure
their children do
without numbers on their arms

Jewball

At first, my fingers
lacked strength and stability,
exactly like my family.

But my Spalding basketball
comforted me all summer long:
a leather sphere with nubby surface,
smells of salty sweat, grime, and blacktop.
The rhythmic sounds of bounce
and the skid of sneakers,
not knowing what would be there
when I returned home.

So, on the hardtop I remained
from morning mist till sunset,
wearing out the soles of black Converse high-tops,
repaired with castoff baseball cards
wrapped in aluminum foil,
fitted between threadbare socks and
the evidence of pivots and push-offs.
I played alone with fantasies of
Coach Holzman, Schayes dominance,
Brown's mastery of the game.
Then, one-on-one, horse, three-on-three
half court, full court pick-up games
winners remain, losers hoping
to regain pride and esteem
lost on the court as good sports,
yet more often without dignity
in loud suburban houses.

We grew taller, learned new skills:
between-the-legs dribbles,
when to chest or bounce pass, pick and roll,
weak-side significance, rebound position
with elbows and shimmy hips,
reverse lay-ups,
scoring at will with a deep, high arching
shot from the corner,
especially from the corners,
escaping a double team
when leaving home.

Elevating for a dunk with funk.
Sometimes a tip-in for the win.
Eventually, spinning the basketball
on my fingertip like a winner's trophy,
straight, strong, and sustained.
Strutting around without a thought
about what awaits after the game.

Harmony/Discordance

listening
a cellist's bow pulling
Bach from crafted hollows
a melodic trance
while sipping tea
eating crustless triangular sandwiches
enveloped by the warmth of community

thinking
I have two homelands
the one I live in
the one that lives inside me
where the cacophony of war
has raged for millennia
passed from one generation to another

feeling
touch of competing rhythms
my peace
my war
harmony
discordance

Our Legacy

While visiting a monument to freedom
Tristram's Dead Sea starlings are alert
as Masada's stoic reminders
of a high rocky fortress
where the business of death
was an ambiguous enterprise
as reports of mass suicide
questioned by modern archeologists

Yet now the commerce of bullets and bombs
continues a Middle East legacy of war
where violence fails resolution

Soon after the killing and the taking
I emailed my Israeli cousins.
We're safe in Tel Aviv
thanks to the Iron Dome,
but in-laws and friends not so fortunate
young children watching parents murdered.

How are you, my cousins ask?
How is your family?
Their polite inquiry stuns.
Has politeness become a modern surprise?

I am sad, worried, concerned, I say.
When will you publish again?
Ordinary questions for ordinary times.
Might the ordinary ever be ordinary again?

Soon, I say, but words are not ammunition.
Yes, but they are our legacy.

Klezmer

The geometry of a festive room
includes the area of a dance floor
the volume of the breaths we synced
while holding each other
listening to the frantic pulse
of klezmer music, howling clarinets
describing the tragedy of our remembrances
the comedy of our lives, wisdom
of collective stories

A Zone of Interest

With your manicured lawns,
scrubbed floors and stolen clothes,
stripped from the not yet dead,
you kept up appearances.

Trains unloaded their breathing cargo,
the furnaces glowed at night,
while house Jews scoured
your sink and tub
of offending ash.

You endured the gunshots,
screams, the horror of inhumanity
with the shroud of your
presumed humanity.

The cultivated cruelty,
not the pictured movie banality,
is a zone of interest
fertilized like flowers
in your greenhouse
with gardens a wall away
from your killing factory.

Dirt

In a cab, the Arab driver asks,
"Where are you from?"
"America"
"Are you a Jew?"
"Yes," I respond.
"May I ride in your cab?"
"Of course, welcome."
He shows me pictures
of his wife and children
with the pride of any
family man.
He drops me off at Yad Vashem
where I cry in Remembrance.

Whose soil washed upon these Middle Eastern shores?
Was the Mediterranean playing a cruel hoax?
Or the Jordan River leading to a dying
Dead Sea, where allegedly holy acts took place?
This land, a crossroads for commerce
and debated truths, for thousands of years,
millions and millions of countless tears.

When I visited Israel during a lull,
the Quarters of Jerusalem filled
with the business of shops and living,
meandering among ancient, stone pathways ...
shofars, rosaries, prayer mats, pomegranates,
the spicy scent of oxtail stew,
hummus, and pita ...
cultures kept their peaceful
separate ways, disparaging the cruelty of leaders
who manipulate and slay for power and control.

Taxis are safety nets,
places where differences
are shared like a scrapbook.

The Cobbler

Long after the beast burned through
like a rabid overheated blast furnace
leaving behind a shell of masonry walls
and the memory of clay and kiln
where kinder fire and quiet labor
shaped pottery and made art

the spirit of a small place
gutted and cauterized
left abandoned among
twisted artisanal infrastructure
thousands of lives left empty,
homeless, with sad eyes,
the clothes on their backs,
a sense of place lost to the cinders

then you returned
surveying emptiness framed
by masonry walls
you a beacon of hope
securing resources to rebuild
a space for creating beauty again
cobbling together the town's soul

Cornucopia

You are a cornucopia of spring
with colorful and alluring whimsy,
dark exotic eyes inviting a fling,
or so I believed before I could see.
Felicity is so often a trap
with threats hidden in a veneer
like a tropical and fanciful wrap
while a dragonfly whispers in your ear.
Held like a king in your soft fragrant hands,
fooled into believing an easy myth
that feeds an identity, yet commands,
you must make a decision and forthwith:
Keep your own heart true and without regret
or learn to sing in an empty duet.

Time Passes

Sitting on the front porch whiling away
memories of a timepiece by the light
in my bedroom ticking moments by day
and dreams that pass quietly at midnight.
When for some inexplicable reason,
hour and second hands stopped their progression
as though life was skipping a short season
with little more than a brief suggestion
of what causes our hearts to flutter when
minutes fill an emptiness often caused
by a reluctance to engage and then
we found the right answer before we paused.
The key to our sorrow would not unlock
until we just repaired a broken clock.

A Blues Impression

Soldered into stained glass
your countenance a broken spirit
with feathered tears hanging
like forgotten whispers
telling secrets that could not be kept.

There were days we wept
armed with easy promises
lacking the solemnity of oaths
knowing there would be a time
when singing the blues
would be a discordant rhyme.

One Note

A cacophony of sounds
threatening the house
like wild hounds.

The concertmaster
tuning the chaos,
avoiding disaster,
creating order,
tamed and ready
with no disorder.

An overture's boom
fills the room.

The Temporary

A bouquet of blue
is an illusion
a best kept secret
a desire, a wish
a love of something
that doesn't exist
in our shared nature.

Fallen from a burst of sunshine
warming our hearts
with the temporary
the temporary glow
it's always the temporary.

On the Likelihood of Aliens

For some, descending light can be
a welcoming curiosity
for answers and possibilities
a confirmation of a future

For others, fear of the unexplained
the threat of alien invasion
light is a glare
a scare with no resolution
something to fear and avoid

Second comings are universal myths
combinations of doubt and hope
wishful thinking
wanting to hold a center
maintaining order
curiosity begging forgiveness

Sons, golems, red cows,
avatars on white horses
mortal inventions
sanctifiers and purifiers
unknowns arriving to save our souls
bearing false promises
when the only light is love

I Lost My Way on the Way to the Monastery

I lost my way
on the way
to the monastery

it was easy
listening to flickers
flickering with a rat-a-rat
like miniature jackhammers

or catching the early morning
scent of cinnamon doughnuts
wafting across the harbor

sometimes staring into
an evening sky
blistered by expanding infinity

all straight lines bend
with the gravity of imagination
the randomness of events
deconstructing predictive
intentions of our own inventions

yet there it is
a place to meditate
the irony of place

Captive by Belief

We were held captive by belief,
a trap often set by faithful
thinking the unknown brought relief.
We were held captive by belief,
regardless of how brief the grief
or a sense of feeling grateful.
We were held captive by belief,
a trap often set by faithful.

Shadows/Daylight

Before

there was daylight,

we disappeared inside

each other's shadows.

GLOSSARY
(the order terms appear in the poems)

shul	A synagogue
putz	A stupid or worthless person
aliyoth	The honor of being called upon to read from the Torah
mishpachah	A Jewish family or social unit including close and distant relatives
mazel tov	A Jewish phrase expressing congratulations or wishing good luck
bubbe	A grandmother; an elderly person
hora	A traditional Israeli circle dance
zaide	Yiddish for grandfather
Baruch atah Adonai Eloheinu	Blessed are You, Lord our God, Ruler of the Universe
boychik	Term of endearment for a young man; boy
nu	How are things? What's new?
klezmer	Traditional eastern European Jewish music
golems	In Jewish legend, a clay figure brought to life by magic

Barry Vitcov lives in Ashland, Oregon, with his wife and exceptionally brilliant standard poodle. His poetry and short stories have appeared in a variety of publications, including *EAP: The Magazine, Literary Yard, The Scarlet Review, Fiction on the Web, Labyrinth, Mobius Blvd., Black Sheep, Dark Horses, The Jefferson Journal,* and *The Rapids.*

He has previously had four books published by Finishing Line Press, a collection of poetry, *Where I Live Some of the Time* (2021); a collection of short stories, *The Wilbur Stories & More* (2022); a chapbook collection of poems *Structures* (2024); and a novella *The Boy with Six Fingers* (2025). FLP will also be publishing a collection of short stories *Unknown & Other Stories* (2026).